Reasons I Can't Sleep

Alyssa Vaccariello

Since I was old enough to remember, I have never been able to sleep at night.

I have also never been able to give a solid answer to anybody when they ask me why.

This book is a compilation of thoughts, anxiety, heartache, nostalgia, and realizations that worked their way out of my head onto this paper in the hours I couldn't sleep. It holds years of writing about could haves and shouldn't haves, yesterdays and somedays, nightmares and dreams.

These are the reasons I can't sleep.

Nightmares

Of time moving too fast, healing moving too slow, anxiety that can't be silenced and words that shouldn't have been.

He falls asleep right when his head hits the pillow.
Every morning he asks how I slept and I say,
"I'm still tired."
But this isn't the kind of tiredness you sleep off at lunch.

It's the kind of tiredness you get from carrying around a
shield and armor in your head all day,
Fighting off every voice that's telling you that you're not
good enough and to give up.

It's the kind of tiredness you get from years of tossing and
turning from crunching the numbers,
Weighing your scale of "what ifs" and regrets and deciding
which is heavier.

It's the kind of tiredness you get from a lifetime of
dragging worry like a weight on your ankle,
Creating made up scenarios and mourning those who are
still alive.

He falls asleep right when his head hits the pillow.
And I hate him for how easy he makes it look.
Not just sleeping,
But living.

I have a confession to make.
I always say I hate sleeping next to people and would
rather sleep alone,
That it's more comfortable and way too crowded
when I share a bed.
The truth is, I hate sleeping next to people because
then you can't sleep without them.
I hate sleeping next to people because when they're
gone so is your peace and comfort.
I hate sleeping next to people because now I'm alone
again at 2 am adjusting 2 pillows under the sheet next
to me so that maybe they'll feel like your body when
I roll over.

- You left me as empty as your side of the bed

In my dream last night I saw you,
And our lips could finally meet.
But I woke up to a world between us,
Where there used to be a sheet.

I wonder if he truly cares about what goes on inside
my head,
Or if he only cares how good I am at giving it.
I wonder if he can tell the days when the weight feels
too heavy on my shoulders,
Or if he only can tell the days when it looks too heavy
on my hips.
I wonder if he knows how passionate about writing I
am,
Or if he only wants to know how passionate about
riding him I am.
I wonder if he wants to tenderly grasp my heart,
Or if he just wants to tenderly grasp my chest that
covers it.

*- Does he want to learn what's inside of me or
just feel it?*

I crave to be understood the way I strive to understand people.

When I'm interested in someone I want to crawl inside their head.

I indulge in their favorite playlists, reading between the lines of each lyric.

I ask them their personality type so I can scroll through pages of explanations for their actions.

I analyze their astrological chart with a fine tooth comb to see who the stars destined them to be.

I place their love languages, childhood trauma, and remains of the past into a textbook and study them cover to cover.

I've accepted that I'll never be understood the way I understand people.

They indulge in my contagious laughter but go silent when it turns to anxiety or darkness.

They ask me about my trauma to see what boundaries I'll let them push.

They analyze my Instagram to see how my tits and hips compare to the other girls in their feed.

They place my insecurities, flaws, and visible traits into a box that they can push under the bed until it's relevant to dig out to prove a point.

- Am I destined to only be the artist and never the muse?

They convinced us we need to take up less space, be so small we could disappear, to be "beautiful."
They convinced us that hook up culture was to our benefit under the false claims of it being "liberating."
So we squeeze at our sides and our stomach until they're red and sore thinking of how much better we'd look if we could rip those parts of us off entirely.
We bite on pillows face down while choking back tears from pain, we get out of their beds and cry in the bathroom, we leave feeling more used than the towel on the floor that he wiped himself off with.
Then, we hold onto the days we look better in the mirror because we haven't eaten in a few.
We hold onto the nights he brought us a glass of water after using our body as a blow up doll.
We look for connection in one-sided beneficial relationships and we look for our worth in what they think of our bodies,
Then we wonder why this "female empowerment" doesn't feel so empowering and this "beauty" feels like a disorder.

I learned in chemistry that when something hot touches something cold, it doesn't just warm it up. There is an exchange of heat, causing each one to be changed by the other.

I was warm, and you were cold. I thought I could make you warm, too.

We touched and I heated you up, using my adoration as a matchstick and my entire self as the flame.

We touched and you gave me chills, using your words as ice picks and my heart as a target.

I didn't realize that trying to change you was going to cause me to change too.

I guess our chemistry made me forget what I learned in class.

I'm the "fun party girl."

I go out every night and convince everyone to take shots, then I wipe my tears in the bathroom stall when I take too many and my mind forgets my name but remembers his.

I dance on the chairs and make everyone laugh while I go home and lay on the bedroom floor muffling cries into pillows to avoid my pain disturbing anybody else.

I fill people up from my empty carafe and then sit awake using the light of the moon to look for all of the missing parts of me.

But at least I'm the "fun party girl."

I'm afraid that it just doesn't make any sense,
How you slid down my throat, got stuck in my chest,
Now I'm reliant on you to make me feel my best,
From our first night together I knew I'd be obsessed.

You show me the best parties and clubs in town,
People always like me more whenever you're around,
My life revolves around you and as bad as it sounds,
What if I don't know how to have fun when I put you
down?

But as soon as you leave I'm surrounded by silence,
My thoughts just consist of self-inflicted violence,
I try to change but I don't know how to fight this,
When you're everywhere, who can I look to for
guidance?

- Liquor, I think you're just making me sicker

I've done so many things I always wanted to do,
So many things we always talked about.
I wonder if you've seen or heard about me.
I wonder what comes to your mind if you have.
I wonder if you're happy for me,
Or if you're sad you aren't a part of it.

I wonder if you can't decide between the two,
Because I can't.

To his new girlfriend…

You probably don't know who I am or anything about
me.
Our photos have been deleted, evidence erased.
But you have still seen me. You see me all the time.

In the man standing in front of you, you're seeing
years and pieces of me, ripped out and molded
together to try and build him into a better person.
In the arms you feel safest in, you're seeing tattoos I
helped sketch and place there.
In the loving messages you receive, you're seeing
words that were tried on me first.
In the lies that are sure to follow, you're seeing
manipulation that was perfected at my expense.
In the tragedy that he's been through, you're seeing
memories that I held him through like a baby in my
lap.

So while you don't know who I am, or anything about
me,
You love so many parts of me that I'll never see
again,
Because they all went into making him the man that
you get to love now.

- His first love

I'm so anxious about the future
It distracts me from the now
Scared I'll have to live without you
And I have no idea how.

This month, it's officially going to be 10 years since I turned 16.
10 years since I was so excited to drive a car.
10 years since my first heartbreak and first drunk mistake.
10 years since 26 seemed like a lifetime away.

This month, it's officially going to be 20 years since I turned 6.
20 years since my biggest decision was which flower dress to wear to school.
20 years since my parents taught me how to ride a bike, telling me that I could take the training wheels off whenever I'm ready but that they'd be right there if I ever fall.
20 years since I had no idea how they'd tell me that many times in my life since, and it would have nothing to do with bikes.

This month, I'll tell them how thankful I am for the birthday card and how much I can't wait to see them when I'm home for the holidays.
And this month I won't tell them how badly I wish I could still turn around from the end of the street,
To see them waving like they did
20 years ago when they taught me to ride a bike and 10 years ago when they taught me to drive a car.

- Mom and Dad, I still need training wheels

Prince Eric didn't ignore Ariel so he could scroll through pictures online of skinnier mermaids with different colored hair than hers.

Prince Phillip didn't take advantage of Sleeping Beauty's sedated body because he felt entitled to please himself at her expense.

The Beast didn't dismiss Belle's interests, passions, and books she loved...he gave her library full of them.

Prince Charming didn't let Cinderella walk out of his life and not bat an eye, he knocked on every door in the kingdom until he found her.

So what am I supposed to tell 5-year-old me about the "Princes" I've suited?

That I don't think she's deserving of the love she grew up yearning for?

- She's still inside me, believing in Disney fairytales but choosing to read tragedies

When we think of "love" we envision images of:
Roses, butterflies, sunsets, fairytales and dreams.

But sometimes, love is loving someone after the roses
have wilted and the thorns have left you bloody.
Love is realizing the butterflies in the pit of your
stomach were actually anxiety.
Love is taking a handful of sleeping pills to kill those
"butterflies."
Love is not knowing when the sun set because you
spent all day lying on the bathroom floor.
Love is more of a Grimm Brothers' fairytale than a
Disney one.
Love is waking up sobbing from a nightmare they
showed up in again.

So why don't those images ever come to mind when
we think of the word "love"?

You said you had a long day and I can only imagine how exhausting it is for you,
Walking around convincing people you're something else all day long.
Then, you have to come home and unzip yourself from the top of your head to your toes and hang up the nice-guy persona on a coat rack by the door until you head back out tomorrow.

How'd I get so lucky to be the only one who gets to see the demon underneath every evening?

Some days, I wake up loving you and fall asleep
hating you.
The hardest part is not knowing which you deserve
more.
Not knowing if I'm imagining the bad in you,
Or if I'm imagining the good in you,
Or if I'll always have to accept the one to get the
other.

- Am I romanticizing the good times,
or dramatizing the bad?

I've never been someone who was motivated by
rejection.
When I didn't make the team I wanted, I didn't try
harder for the next year. I gave up.
When girls were mean to me in school, I didn't
defend myself. I stopped going to school.
When I didn't get into the college I wanted, I didn't
study harder. I applied to an easier one.

But with love, I've allowed myself to take rejection as
a challenge to prove my worth.
I've accepted betrayal, abuse, lies and disrespect as a
gift box carefully wrapped with a bow that spells out
"try harder."
Try harder and they'll respect you. Try harder and
they'll stop lying to you.
Try harder and you can fix them,
Try harder and they'll love you the way you love
them.

I've never been someone who was motivated by
rejection.
Until it came from your lips.

"Hey babe, do you want to do something tonight?
We could go to that new restaurant, get a drink, see a movie…"
"Sorry I had a really stressful day at work."

And practically within the same breath

"Where are you going?"
"Oh me and the guys are going to get drinks, big game is on tonight."

And then you wonder why one day you check if she's still on that shelf you left her on to see she's dusted herself off, looked in the mirror, and walked out the door.

> *- What you take for granted, one man*
> *will take to the altar*

I hate the way it feels every time you say my name,
I hate how nobody can ever make it sound the same.

I hate that your fingerprints are stained into my skin,
I hate that it's impossible to let someone new in.

I hate that I forgave you for every single lie,
I hate that no amount of vodka makes me forget, but
still I try.

I hate that if I fall asleep I dream about your touch,
I hate that none of these things seem to bother you
that much.

I want to set it all on fire.
I want to ignite these sheets, this bed,
Full of your sweat, love, and lies.
I've tried to drown it,
But my tears can't wash away the things these walls
have seen.
They repeat your whispered promises to me every
night,
Never letting me forget about the nights we lit up this
room with passion,
Instead of rage.

I loved all the darkest parts of you.
I fell into your deepest caves and didn't even try to
bring a flashlight.
I walked hand in hand with your demons.
I became so intertwined with them, I couldn't tell
which ones were yours and which ones were mine
anymore.
I held your past trauma in my hands until it cut them
up and mixed my blood with yours.
Every terrible thing you'd done, every mental
struggle, every secret from the past,
I loved them all. I loved them so much I gave them a
home in me.
And they stayed, even after you left.

- Is that why she gets the light parts of you now?

What else can I do?
I go out with friends,
I even go out with guys.
I laugh at their jokes and I smile like I mean it.
I picked up some hobbies and I stay busy.
I count back the days and months since I've last seen
you to try and track my progress,
But I think that's the opposite of progress.
I cry when I can, and hope that every ounce of pain I
let out will mean less that I have to carry.
The time won't go any fucking faster,
And the hole in my chest can't be filled with fake
smiles at men who don't know anything about me.
But then again, did you?
What else can I do?
What else can I do?
What the fuck else can I do?

I've realized that you can run from your problems
But they'll always catch you.
I get older,
Wiser,
Less trusting,
More experienced,
Move across the damn country,
And all that changes
Is the skyline I'm looking at at 2 am
And the boy who made me stay up this late crying.

I run into new cities,
New arms,
And I still always find my way
Right back here.

If everything that goes around comes around,
And everything that goes up must come down,
Then tell me what the fuck is the point?
You can only write so many words until the page
ends,
Only drink so much until the bottle's empty,
Only love so much until your heart breaks.
We live life looking for the light at the end of the
tunnel,
Or the next high on the rollercoaster…
Until it drops again.
With every mountain you'll have a valley.
Flowers can't grow until a storm hits.
So how the fuck can you tell me not to fear happiness
when I know what's on the other side of it?

We were more than friends and less than lovers,
And then we turned into more than lovers who
weren't even friends half the time,
And now we're less than both.

- The whole point was to end up with
more of you, not less

Last night I couldn't sleep,
And it wasn't because I didn't know what to do
anymore like so many nights before.
It's because I did.

Somehow, it's more comforting to live in the in-
between,
Knowing maybe we shouldn't work it out, but hoping
we do.
In the in-between, there's hope.
In the in-between, there's still a vision of a future,
even if it's blurry.

Knowing what I want to do feels a hell of a lot worse.
There's no denial or shred of hope to grab onto.
I've been here enough times to come to terms with
the disheartening truth that nothing will ever change.

What's even sadder is that I don't even think you'd
argue or put up a fight,
Because you know it as well as I do.
We've both fallen out of the in-between,
And it kind of makes me miss it there.

"Hello."
There's not much to talk about but it's good to hear your voice.
Familiar. Gentle. Raspy.
I know that "hello" is only half-opening dead-bolted doors allowing nothing more than half-conversations.
"How are you?"
"How's your family?"
"How's work going?"
…
"Good."

And we both know it's not good.
I've started to forget the way your eyes wrinkle when you smile and the freckles on your chest I've traced into countless constellations with my fingers.
But none of that seems appropriate to tell you.
So out of fear of forgetting your voice too,
I'll just settle for
"Hello."

I loved him.

My God, I think I loved that boy more than I've ever loved anything.

But 18 years old is awfully young to understand the depths of "forever" and I still wanted... I *needed*...to find myself.

It's been years and I've lost and found myself countless times over but I'll never stop comparing everyone to him.

I found myself here, and he found himself there. And there's nothing more tragic than that.

- In the end, did I lose more than I found?

I always hear the reassurance,
"You aren't asking for too much, you're asking the wrong person."
And that's a nice sentiment, and probably true.
But it completely ignores the fact that you don't want to ask the "right person," you want them to BE the "right person."
You don't want to ask the guy who hit on you at the bar or asks you on a date in your DMs to love you how you want to be loved.
You want to ask the one who sees you cry and doesn't change hoping this time one of those teardrops will fill his hands to the brim so he can finally splash his eyes and clearly see your worth.

- If he were the right one, would you be crying this often?

"I'm a relationship girl,"
I say like it's something to be proud of.
I say it like I should be proud that I don't spend a
night trying to convince a man to want me,
Instead I spend years at a time doing it.
I say it like I should be proud that a lot of people
haven't seen my body,
Instead ones who did saw beneath the skin to my
beating heart and left me more open and exposed than
any one night stand.
I say it like I should be proud that I don't date
casually,
Instead I pin all my future plans on their potential and
come out 2 years older and twice as broken as I was
before.

- I wish I wasn't a "relationship girl"

Smiling
Flirting
Going to dinner
Watching a movie
Having a drink
"I'm not like that"
"Can we take things slow"
Nervous laughter
Pushing away hands
"Stop"
"Please"
"No"
"Ow"
"Stop"
"Stop"
"Stop"
"Stop"
Silence

- Things that don't mean yes

Supposedly every 7 years all of our skin cells are
replaced,
But I don't know if I believe that.
It's been more than that and sometimes I still feel the
hands that I begged not to touch me.
I still feel the pull on clothing that I tried to make
tighter on me.
I still feel the eyes on places I wanted to keep hidden
and I still feel the dread anytime I meet a new man
that they'll touch my new and "clean" skin cells
without my permission.

*- Maybe new skin can't grow over
scars cut that deep*

I don't know how to answer the question, "What's wrong?"

"I'm just sad"

"About what?"

Well, I'm sad about the people I loved and learned just to have them become useless shrines of distant memories. I'm sad I don't remember the swing set at my parents' first house and I'm sad I only see them on holidays. I'm sad about the seasons changing through another year that I didn't accomplish the things I thought I'd have done by now. I'm sad my life is passing me by and half the time I spend it convincing myself I enjoy living. I'm sad I'm not 5 years old about to watch a movie with my family and I'm sad I'm not 15 years old about to meet my first love, I'm sad that instead I'm at the point where I'm convinced I'll never find another because time hasn't been very kind to my heart since then.

"I'm just sad."

"It's just seasonal" I say.
"It's just that time of year."
It's just that time of year where every day starts to
feel the same.
It's just that time of year where nostalgia chains me to
the bed more than the cold.
It's just that time of year where it's always gray
outside my window and inside my head.
It's just that time of year where the sky gets darker
earlier and so do my thoughts.

You fake proposed to me in the bar full of people and swung me around as we kissed.
I thought it was hilarious how excited they got over something that was fake.
But I didn't realize that from the moment I fell for you, I had been doing the same thing as them.

- None of it was real, was it?

When you feel yourself losing your mind, a doctor medicates you to sedate you.

When I feel myself losing my mind, wondering how on Earth I got in this position, my medication is looking back at our old text messages and the things you used to say to me to remind myself that I had every reason to believe you'd be the man you convinced me you were who could love me the way you said you did.

- I didn't make it all up in my head, you put it there

You control me like a ventriloquist.
You tickle my legs and they open for you.
You tap at my heart and it aches for you.
You touch my hands and they reach for you.
You glance at my lips and they smile for you.
You turn from my eyes and they pour for you.
You breathe the air into me,
And you steal it from my lungs.
Do you have any idea how terrifying that is?

I thought we had *passion*.
We'd scream and degrade each other until "slut" and "bastard" became foreplay.
Jealousy danced in our eyes and spite dripped off of our tongues into each others' mouths.
We argued until our own flames engulfed us,
Leaving us to cling to each other among the ashes,
inhaling the smoke of an extinguished love that we had nobody to blame for but ourselves.

- Why has society convinced us that passion and abuse are synonymous?

If I could go back and talk to my younger self
I'd tell her to memorize every inch of the walk to her
locker and every crevice of the boy she shared it with.
I'd tell her to memorize the movie lines her dad
always repeats that drive her insane.
I'd tell her to burn her mom's smile when she walks
through the door into her brain.
I'd tell her to save the smell of the first leaves
changing in September and put it away in a bottle that
she can open from time to time.
I'd tell her she can probably forget her college
lecture, but not to forget so many nights from
drinking too much.
Have a couple shots less, and memorize exactly how
many bricks are between your house and your best
friend's.
I'd tell her to memorize her roommates' footsteps
because the videos won't capture it when you look
back.
I'd tell her to memorize all of the things she takes for
granted to put away for the days she's going to sit in
bed wondering when she forgot the smell of autumn,
how long it took her mom to get to the garage to greet
her after school, or what her dad's favorite TV line is.

It's not until you're halfway through your twenties,
Living across the country from your family,
Alone in the apartment that you pay for on your own
With your full-time job,
Eating dinner by yourself,
That you don't know whether to be proud of yourself
Or to cry.

-Isn't this what I wanted?

When I was young and watched mystery shows like
Scooby Doo,
I always wondered how it was so clear who the
monster was to everybody besides the detective.
"How stupid do they have to be?" I'd think.
Until I fell in love with you,
And I finally understood how they felt.

- Everyone knew you were the monster but me

She always had her head in the clouds.
She'd stare at them for hours.
She never understood how they looked so soft,
comforting, and safe.

Yet they could also roar through the night, producing
storms that could derail entire cities,
And if she were to ever put any real weight on one,

She'd fall right through.

She always had her in the clouds,
Until she met a boy who acted like one.
There at night, gone by morning,
Using his thunder to keep her awake and looking like
a safe, relaxing, place to rest,

But never once catching her.

I don't want to sleep in case I see you there.
I don't want to see your wicked, satanic grin,
Standing there salivating at my suffering.
I don't want to see your agile, gripped hands,
Ready to knock me down a peg if I dare speak up.
I don't want to see your cold, black eyes,
Wandering to other women as I lay here at your feet.

I don't want to sleep in case I see you there.
I don't want to see your charming, angelic smile,
Speaking in sonnets about my beauty.
I don't want to see your strong, familiar hands,
Eager to lift me to the top of a pedestal.
I don't want to see your warm, inviting eyes,
Undressing me before I can do it myself.

- I don't know which version of you is scarier

Every time you get your heart broken, people love to tell you how "this will be a lesson that you're thankful for one day."
"You'll come out so much stronger, wiser, and better from this."
But that gives the person who broke your heart way too much credit.
Well I've gotten to "one day," and I can honestly say I will never be thankful to have experienced the heart-racing, soul-shattering love that you introduced me to.
You taught me lessons I never should've had to learn.
You made self-proclaimed "character development" at the expense of a young girl's perception of herself and of the entire world.
You willingly took everything she had to give until you left her a broken shell of the girl she was when you found her.

Sure, I came out stronger, wiser, and better,
But I would've been strong, wise, and better either way.
I did not need you to traumatize me to get to be the person I am today.

- You don't get any credit for the woman I became despite you

You know you love someone when you turn the pain they cause you into poetry instead of a reason to leave.

Everyone acknowledges how hard it is to move on,
But I rarely hear them talk about how hard it is to
choose not to.
How hard it is to choose to try again,
To choose to work through every issue, concern, and
betrayal,
To be laying on their chest and hear the sound of the
door slamming when they left,
To see their hands and remember where else they've
been,
To tell the guards of your caged up heart to let down
the gates one more time, and watch them sigh as they
do it.

I guess the sting of the needle makes me feel more alive than the softness of a hug.

I guess the frigid cold piercing my eyes and leaving me lost for breath makes me feel more in my chest than the warmth that fills my cheeks when I walk outside on a summer day.

I guess the darkness at 3 am makes me feel more seen than the brightness of the morning.

I guess the uncertainty and anxiety makes me feel like I have something more "special" than security and comfort do.

I guess when they break my heart, I can't blame them for doing what I always knew they would.

- I'm scared I'll never choose a healthy love

Friends love to tell you that "It'll get easier someday."
And sure, it gets easier.
You'll stop gripping your chest from the pain,
hyperventilating into your pillow about him every
night,
But years later something will remind you of him and
you'll quietly cry yourself to sleep.
You'll stop checking his social media every day for
smoke signals posted for you to see and waiting on
the dreaded day he posts a new girl.
But years later you'll stumble across it and it'll still
sting.
You'll stop waiting hopelessly for him to come back,
or to change, or to die without you like he said he
would.
So sure, it will be easier,
But it will never be forgotten.

If this is it,
And I'm destined to spend the foreseeable future
avoiding places you are or hearing about who you're
with now while I watch you forget about me through
our mutual friend's photos,
I want you to know that I really did try.

I'll smirk at your pictures and grimace when someone
brings you up, while clinging to every word as my
only portals into what your life is like now.
I'll roll my eyes and make passive aggressive digs
when I hear your name, while trying to hide the fact
that hearing it made my stomach turn.
I'll act like you're a complete joke while
remembering the ones that we spent years making
together.

I'll act like you're insignificant to hide how painfully
significant you still are to me.

I cried an ocean for you and all it made me realize was how much fun we'd have swimming in it.

Run a marathon hungover
Take 20 shots of warm tequila
Get stranded in the middle of the ocean
Count how many blades of grass are in the entire city
Cut my tongue out and pin it to the fridge
Rip my hair out one strand at a time
Replay every memory while I try and fall asleep
Wake up every morning thinking about you
Watch you forget about me from afar
Know I could stop it all if I wanted to
Know I could stop it all if I put my pride aside

- Things I'd do before telling you I miss you

I've spent years trying to win unseen wars against the
voices in my mind.
I've tried to drown them out with liquor,
Or scare them silent with drugs.
I've held a bag over their heads and tried to suffocate
them from their air supply.
I've killed everything off but their host.
And no matter what I do,
Every single time they come back up gasping for air
The first word out of their mouth
Is your fucking name.

Men will search galleries for something that catches
their eyes.
They'll find the most admired art piece and purchase
it for themselves,
Putting it into a corner in their dimly lit apartment
where nobody can see it.
They'll rope off that part of the room, just so nobody
goes near it.
They'll tell the art that nobody is interested in seeing
it anymore.
They'll make the art believe that it deserves to be in a
dark corner and that it's lucky it was purchased by
anybody at all.

- An insecure man is a woman's biggest threat

Your funeral wasn't beautiful or poetic.
I didn't have any closure or understanding of why it happened,
And you didn't leave any words behind that would help me make sense of it all.
People were laughing at my pain and flocking to your casket before I could even process what had happened,
Grabbing the hands I hadn't yet parted with, kissing the lips I was still waiting for answers from.
I had to draw my own conclusions, give myself closure, wipe my own tears, hug myself through the sleepless nights,
And hold my own memorial service for you,
Every night since you've been gone.

I guess that's what happens when you have to mourn the death of someone who's still very much alive.

I'd like to think you're still burdened by the regret of losing me.
I'd like to think it's grown deep inside you and burned your throat for years.
I'd like to think that you wake up from dreams of me thrashing, just to roll over into her arms and wince when they don't feel like mine.
I'd like to think one day when you watch your future walk down the aisle, a montage of what could have been plays behind your eyes,
And while the audience thinks your tears are for the bride-to-be,
They're really for me.

I'd like to think you have the emotional capacity and undying love for me that I saw in fleeting moments.
In reality, I'm sure I haven't crossed your mind, and certainly not your dreams.
In reality, I'm sure I'm a distant memory.

But I'd like to think I'm not.

I'll probably always look for your face in any
crowded bar,
And hearing that song will take me back to late nights
in your car,
I know every time I've left I haven't gotten very far,
But my heart doesn't have the room for another scar.

For years I've been begging, knowing I don't deserve
this.
How could I be in love with someone who makes me
feel worthless?
Why would you abuse the woman you "love" on
purpose?
I figured if I just kept trying that you'd stop wanting
to hurt this.

And I know you'll never see the damage you've
caused me permanently,
And how seeing myself through your eyes made me
lose my identity,
And how I'd have grabbed the sun right out of the sky
to make you see,
That I'd have taken a bullet for the man who was
holding the gun to me.

I grieve my first love because I didn't just lose him,
I lost that version of myself.
I miss that girl and the love she could give.
I miss her ability to be vulnerable because she didn't
have a reason not to be yet.
I miss the glimmering and naive hope we had that
love really meant forever.

We both learned that the hundreds of love letters to
each other would end up in a box mixed in with
remains of the relationships that would follow,

But it was so nice to still believe that they wouldn't.

I hear the wise advice,
"You never know the value of a moment until it
becomes a memory."
But that's never been the case with me.

For as long as I can remember, I've been pathetically
gripping the hands of time, bargaining with them,
trying to spin them backwards or stop them entirely.

My hands are sore and blistered from how hard I try
and hold onto moments to stop them from becoming
memories.

When I was a little kid I ran away from home.
What that really meant was that I sat on the side of
the house long enough to make my parents realize I
was gone and go insane trying to find me.
I didn't really want to leave, but I "ran away" to know
if they'd miss me.

That's what I was doing when I left you, too.

- Except you didn't come looking for me

Being a lover hasn't really worked out for me.
My heart decided it wanted a break.
I became numb.
Detached.
Casual.
I don't let him see inside my mind, but I don't care if
he sees inside my shirt.
I don't get butterflies when he kisses me, but I also
don't get stabbing chest pain when I don't hear from
him.
I don't get moved by his words, but I also don't get
shattered by them.
I don't get loyalty, but I also don't get betrayal.
I don't get love, but I also don't get heartbreak.

My heart decided it wanted a break,
And I don't know if it'll ever go back to work again.

- Is feeling no pain worth feeling no love?

My heart used to be ready, warm, on fire.
It's frozen over, an icy sculpture of what it once was.
I thought this was a form of protection,
But if they drop a heart made of ice it will shatter.
If they drop a heart made of flames it will engulf
everything around it.

- Maybe being colder doesn't make me any stronger

Dreams

*Of moments and people I wanted to hold onto longer,
and strength and realizations that helped me hold
onto life tighter.*

Anxiety and nightmares aren't the only reasons I can't sleep at night.
I can't sleep at night because I'm busy piecing together years of experience to come to realizations.
I can't sleep at night because I'm dreaming of 20 different ideas I want to juggle into a plan by tomorrow.
I can't sleep at night because I'm having conversations in my mind with people to avoid having them in person.
I can't sleep at night because I'm inspired by how the moon shines through the darkness into my bedroom window like I want to be able to do for so many people with my words.
I can't sleep at night because the hours after midnight are for those who feel deeper than the rest of the world.
And feeling that deep is a superpower, not a weakness.

I started to build this world for myself,
Where if I'm hurting there's something to help.
It takes away all of the pain that I've felt,
And I can control every hand that I'm dealt.

Everyday feels like summer in this place I call home.
I'm learning to love the feeling of being alone,
And that words of reassurance still work when they're
my own,
And I'm strong enough to rebuild myself bone by
bone.

This beautiful place that exists in my mind,
Has shown me that nothing will fix me but time.
So I'll sit and I'll write, and I'll cry, and I'll rhyme,
And the world will keep going and so will I.

I'll keep visiting this place every night in my dreams,
Because reality isn't really all that it seems.
And one of these days I'll wake up finally free,
In love with the scars, all the bruises, and me.

I was never more relieved than when you showed up
in my dream.
Not because I wanted to see you in my sleep,
But because for as long as I can remember,
You've only been in my nightmares.

In my nightmares you haunt me like a demon.
You make me relive my pain and dump salt in my
wounds,
Throwing my hands off of my eyes to make me watch
every detail and thrust.

In my dream, you didn't have a single powerful
quality.
You apologized, for years of pain I've had to heal
without your help,
Scattering your own insecurities across the floor.

I was never more relieved than when you showed up
in my dream.
Because finally you were just a boy I once loved,
Who probably loved me back more than I remember,
And not the mystical beast that my pain turned you
into.

- My mind finally took your power away

The silence is uncomfortable,
But so are the hands of someone not meant for you.

- Learn to be comfortable in loneliness

I see you in the lights from the airplane windows,
Beautiful from far away, but get closer and they're
just ordinary houses and storage units,
Damaged and full of ghosts from the past.
But when I'm in the sky I like to close my eyes and
imagine all of the things that I know will never
happen on the ground.
I play the song that reminds me of you and allow
myself to daydream of a world where the haunted,
broken house on the ground isn't full of ghosts.
Instead it's full of our wedding photos and a navy
blue couch we picked out to perfectly match the rug.
And to the left of the couch is the kitchen where we
slow dance at night and sneak spoonfuls of each
other's ice creams.
It has a king-sized bed where the cat sleeps between
us and a bathroom where we leave love notes on the
mirror when it steams from the shower.
It holds a painfully and beautifully mundane life,
One that I'd have never grown tiresome of with you
by my side,
One where each ordinary idiosyncrasy would always
be extraordinary to me.
But then the song ends. And the plane lands.
And as it hits the ground, so do my dreams of a life
where you and I could be anything more than
strangers with a lot of history.

- I'll see you from the windows on the next flight

I still reach for you in bed, but only on nights when I drink too much.

I still listen to your old voicemails, but only a couple times a month.

I hope we get to talk about it all someday, even if it's not for another year.

I hope you still think of me sometimes, even if it's in ways I'll never hear.

I thought there'd be countless people I'd have deep connections with in my lifetime,
But in reality there will only be a few, if that.
I realize it every time I see one of those few again.
When our eyes meet, and something in my body relaxes because it's recognizing that this person has been home for me,
In this lifetime and probably past ones.
It knows that parts of me now live within that person forever,
Parts of me I gave to them long ago, parts I haven't seen since.
It recognizes old mannerisms and memories that were given up in the loss of each other.
It will always only find a bittersweet comfort, though.
Because while the connection will always be there, it will only ever show itself in fleeting moments, too quick to grasp and put away for later.
So I guess I'm bound to forever touching it when I can and graciously allowing it to leave after,
Reminding myself that it's a positive I was ever lucky enough to form such a beautiful connection, rather than a negative that I may have to wait until the next lifetime to ever find it again.

I think when you love someone,
I mean love someone with everything you have,
The love doesn't ever fully go away.
I think it stays within us, with nowhere to go.
So we pour it into new containers and change its form
since we can't drain it out of us all together.
We watch as it morphs itself into containers shaped
like hatred, grief, and if you're lucky one day,
friendship.

- Real love doesn't go away, it just changes forms

You offered me the world, but it was a world that you
had built for me.
It was safe and solid with no threats or danger.
I knew I'd never get hurt there.
I knew it was full of love and loyalty,
And late nights drinking wine and eating banana
bread,
And someone to always stop to pet every dog with
me,
And always tuck me back in after I had nightmares.
And in this world I knew I'd always be content and
comfortable.
And your world is so beautiful.
But I had to learn how to build my own.
And someday you will offer someone the world and
they will smile to the sun and accept in such a way
that makes you understand why I couldn't.

- I still visit your world in my dreams

I just want to say thank you.
You shed light and hope into my darkest, deepest
cracks.
I went from not wanting to see the future, to planning
every detail of it right down to the names of our kids,
the colors of our walls, and the endless adventures
we'd have.
I never went to sleep thinking that I wasn't enough.
I never doubted myself,
Or you.
You are the type of person that this world needs more
of,
The type of person to make me believe in love, trust,
and humanity all over again.
Thank you for saving me.
Thank you for opening your heart and hands to me.
Thank you for loving me when I couldn't love
myself.
And thank you for never giving up,
Even after I did.

I may have been the one who closed the door on us, but I still look out the window to check if you're there.

You know that feeling you get when you're about to do something that you know you shouldn't?
The rush of adrenaline, the excitement of uncharted territory.
It's the feeling you get when you sneak out at 2am on a school night.
It's the feeling you get when you skip school to get high with your friends.
It's the feeling of getting absolutely hammered but knowing you have work at 7 am.
It's the feeling when your eyes dilate, and your bloodstream fills with drugs,
And you know you're about to have a high reward with a much higher risk.

That's what falling in love with you felt like.

Sometimes I think the relationships that didn't work out are the most romantic.

It was romantic when we were together, but it was also hard.

There were fights, bickering, little annoyances we had with each other.

There was resentment that would still loom above our heads if we were together.

But now, as years have passed since, I feel nothing but gratitude for you.

We still exchange glances that hold adoration, for all that our love taught and gave us.

All the bitterness we held while trying to make things work has blown away with the wind of time.

We can dance, laugh, and occasionally talk about "remember when."

We'll always have pieces of each other that nobody else will for the rest of our lives as we continue down our parallel paths.

So call me crazy, but I find it pretty romantic to know that while we weren't the best for each other, we still wish the best for each other.

- Promise to look after the pieces of me that you have, and I promise to look after yours

Years have passed,
Planets have realigned,
People have died and been born again
Since we fell apart.
Yet you always reappear in my mind
Like the first drop of rain after a drought,
The first glimpse of the sun after a harsh winter,
Gone but never far enough to forget how good it
feels.
Never far enough to forget the thirst the rain
quenches,
And the warmth the sun breathes back into our skin as
the flowers look up to greet it.
I can't help but wonder if that's how it would feel
with the return of you too.

Let's do it again, but get it right this time.
Let's take every hurt and betrayal and lie them to rest in the middle of the room alongside the past versions of ourselves.
We'll have a funeral for them and instead of bringing flowers to it, let's bring everything we've learned since.
We'll make love on the burial ground of our mistakes and rebirth something twice as beautiful from it.
Let's pick back up the pen and write a sequel to the love story that ended far too soon.

- I know we have a better ending than that

I've dreamed about my fairytale wedding since I was
a little girl.
I'll have the perfect dress built for a princess, with my
hair in loose curls falling down my back.
There will be pink and white roses flooding the room
in the most ethereal way I've ever seen.
I'll be standing across from a man who was written
for me out of a romance novel.
I have almost all of it planned perfectly right down to
the seating arrangement.
The one detail I can't figure out exactly, is what part
of the vows you're going to interrupt to tell me you
object and haven't been able to go a single day
without thinking about me?

*- I'll leave those dreams in an instant to live
one out with you*

The voices in my head have been mesmerized by you.
They come to standstill at the sound of your voice.
Your laugh sends chills down their spine.
Your smile brings them to their knees.
You have penetrated the darkest depths of me, and are
reminding my demons of when they were angels.

He said,

"Falling in love with her is like jumping out of an airplane.

One second you're standing on two feet and the next you're thrown from 12,500 feet up, second guessing if you should've done it. There's literally a million ways it could go wrong. But if everything goes just right, the parachute opens on time, you skillfully maneuver through the wind, and you land on a target that's ready to catch you...

Then you'll be chasing a high like that for the rest of your life."

Is it better to know a lot about a little, or to know a little about a lot?
I know a lot about you.
I know a lot about the way you look when you're choking back your feelings.
I know a lot about your childhood and the reasons you think the way that you do.
I know a lot about how you feel in the mornings when you want to be extra close to me and extra far from work.
I know a lot about how many steps it takes to get from my car to your door and how many times I've found myself taking them even when I knew I probably shouldn't have.

So I guess I don't know if it's better to know a lot about a little or a little about a lot,
But what's the point of knowing a little bit about everything if that means I wouldn't get to know a lot about you?

I know that wherever *you* and *I* end up,
Wherever *you* and *I* go from here,
That won't be where *we* are.

Where we are is so much more beautiful. We are still kissing in the car looking up at fireworks through the sunroof. We are still dancing together while we brush our teeth. We are holding hands and sneaking off from the crowd to make out in the back of the bar. We are laying in bed ignoring our emails and laughing about the thought that we were ever with anybody else.

We will forever live in those days. *You* and *I* may not be, but *we* will be there whenever I flip back the pages. I'll find comfort in seeing us there when I need to be reminded how *we* are doing. I know right now we're there, smiling through kisses having no idea that you and I could ever be in separate stories.

We will always be there. Even if *you* and *I* are here.

When I go to my happy place I think of you,
Back to a time when your eyes and the sky were
bright blue.
And I know we've moved on, and there's no more
forever,
But on my worst days, it's you I remember.

I got tired of saying "I love you" just because it was my only way of maybe hearing it back.
I got to the point of showing appreciation for you just in hopes it would be returned,
And coming onto you just in hopes you'd start lusting over me like you did in the beginning.
Affection stopped being genuine and became a consistent attempt at an example.
I got tired of giving my love to you in hopes you'd mimic it,
When I should've just given it to myself instead.

*- Why teach a middleman how to deliver the
message when I can just do it myself*

I'd rather be the one that got away than the one that
stayed.
I'd rather be the one who haunts him than the one
who holds him.
I'd rather be the kiss that scorched him than the one
that soothes him after a bad day.
I'd rather be the one who left a scar on his heart than
the one who is staying up at night trying to mend it,
Using its damage to justify his actions.
I'd rather be the one he broke into a million pieces
than the one who thinks he's a "good guy."
I'd rather be the one he never sees again than the one
he sees every morning.

Because he will always take for granted the one he
has, and he will always romanticize the one he lost.

- Men can miss you far more than they can love you

Losing you made me realize that I rarely mourn our
memories,
Or even you.
I mourn the idea of you I created.
I mourn the future I built in my head by using your
best moments, fragile promises, and false hope.
I mourn the potential I saw in you,
The life I saw for us,
And the hope I saw in me.

Losing you made me realize that I mourn beautiful
things that didn't exist in you,
But they existed in me.
My mind and love are what made you special,
And I get to use them to make myself special now.

As life changes we grow,
We outgrow,
We lose each other in the transition.
I can't say I'm mad anymore, because I'm not.
I don't want you to suffer how I have,
It doesn't make me happy seeing you hurting.
I want you to continue to grow,
I want you to thrive.
I want you to do everything you possibly can in one lifetime,
Everything you've ever wanted to do.
I hope you meet people that take your breath away,
But never your smile.
I want you to see the most beautiful places the world can show you.
Then, at those moments where you're full of genuine happiness and wonder,
I want you to think of me.

*- I hope you see parts of me in
the beautiful moments*

To her ex…

I wanted to let you know that she's doing just fine,
I've never known a woman could be so divine,
I get luckier each morning that I see her smile shine,
And if it weren't for you, she may have never been mine.

So thank you for causing her those sleepless nights,
If you hadn't she probably wouldn't hold me as tight,
I see some of your damage come out when we fight,
But I'll never let a day go without saying "I love you goodnight."

And even though she's the strongest person I know,
I'll be here to hold her up if she can't on her own.
I'll always lift her crown and keep her on her throne.
You'd be amazed if you saw how much she's grown.

- Her next

I've always had a problem with making ordinary
moments extraordinary in my head.
Or maybe it's a blessing.
Because to you, I was lying on your chest falling in
and out of sleep.
An ordinary interaction with nothing noteworthy
about it.
But to me, I was listening to your heart beat in one
ear and my own in the other,
Creating a song in my head that strung together both
of our rhythms,
Coordinating my breath like an instrument to help
them sync up and beat together.

*- I'd rather make a symphony of
silence than not hear the music*

One day, by happenstance, I'll meet the one who
makes me thankful for every heartbreak,
Tear-stained pillow,
Dagger in my chest,
And ruined memory.

He'll want to crawl inside my brain so badly that he'll
indulge in every song I like,
Book I recommend,
Interest I briefly mention,
And dream I have.

He'll read my poetry and worship my mind.
He'll hold my armor when I'm tired and allow me to
be soft.
He'll help me fill every space instead of shrinking me
to fit perfectly into his checked boxes,
Making me thank the universe for those whose boxes
I didn't check.

> *- I wanted to check their boxes so badly I*
> *didn't realize they never checked mine*

There's nothing better than the very beginning stages
of a relationship.
I don't know if it's because I'm excited to get to
know them, or if it's because I can still imagine them
as who I want them to be rather than who they are.

- I've always loved being creative

When he's left you searching corners of your eclipsed mind for the light he once saw in you,
When he's left you lifting up old boxes trying to find where you put the "fun, cool girl" he fell in love with,
Take my hand.

You are still her and I will remind you every time you forget.

- Your worth didn't disappear when his admiration did

Buying each other flowers and making each other
care packages
Baking cakes just to write something on it with icing
that will make them smile
Packing picnics to share
Going on long drives to nowhere
Singing so loud our throats hurt
Sitting and enjoying the silence when they do
Writing love notes to men we base years of our
conversations around
Crying in each other's beds when they don't love us
back
Discussing replaceable names with an irreplaceable
person
Learning we can live without men but never live
without each other
Spending our time looking for soul mates while we're
sitting right next to one

- Platonic soul mates

One year ago…

I have my head in my hands outside the bar.
My entire body is shaking from how cold it is.
I'm sitting here crying right where you left me.
I'm calling an Uber and wondering what they'll think
of picking me up on the street at 1 am alone.
I place my hand over my arm to feel where you
grabbed it, the faint throbbing reminding me it wasn't
just in my imagination.
This can't be the love they talk about in books and
movies.
This can't be the love I deserve.

Today...

I have my head in my hands outside the bar.
My entire body is shaking from laughter.
I'm sitting here re-telling a story that gets funnier
every time.
I'm calling our friends inside the bar to ask if they
can just sneak us in the back.
I place my hand into theirs and we run to the dance
floor because they're playing my favorite song.
This feels like the love they talk about in books and
movies.
This feels like the love I deserve.

*- I stopped looking for love in the wrong
places and realized it was right in front of me*

We work our entire lives to achieve this
institutionalized, diluted idea of happiness.
Get good grades to get into a good college.
Get a degree to get a good job.
Get a good job to get a lot of money,
That you can spend on a big house with expensive
liquor that you can pour while you consequently
complain about your job.
I decided long ago I'd rather be rich in memories.
Emotions.
Experiences.
Poetry.
Love.

Things I can't hold onto, but things that will hold
onto me.

There is writing with specific formats,
Double-spaced and punctual,
Lifeless. Factual. Forced.
Then there is writing that propels itself from your
fingertips with a life of its own,
A life that you've given it.
Words spill and crash onto the pages like waves from
the depths of your mind,
With the strength to dismantle entire cities.
Entire beings.
Writing is a way of taking your experiences, your
emotions,
And turning them into a storm.
Powerful. Painful. Real

I'm a skeptic.
I've never believed in religion, or Santa, or things I
can't see.
But I've always had full faith in one force:
Karma.
I've seen her myself.
She gives me closure and reassurance.
I find closure in knowing she'll always visit those
who deserve her, and reassurance in the fact that I
take that as something to look forward to rather than
something to dread.

I never understood why grudges get such a bad
reputation.
"Move on, let it go, forget about it."
I hold my grudges like a suit of armor,
Not like a heavy chain around my ankle.
They don't hold me back or weigh me down,
They empower me, protect me, and reassure me,
That I'll keep moving forward, even stronger, past
every betrayal.

I just want you to know I notice.
I notice that you are actively working to undo
generational trauma and give me the love you didn't
receive from your own father.
I notice that it's not always easy for you, and I notice
the pain in your eyes when you remember.
I notice that you are everything he couldn't be and
more.
I notice that I am lucky every single day to be an
extension of the man I admire more than anything.
I notice that you set the bar so high, no other man
could dream of reaching it.
I notice that this life has not always been kind to you.
And I notice that you've never reciprocated.

- I notice, Dad

I had a dream where I got to meet 16 year old me.
She feels like nobody understands her.
Not the people at school, not her "friends," certainly
not her parents.
She told me about all of the pain she's going through
and how nobody takes her depression seriously
because they think teenagers are dramatic.
She told me she can't go another day feeling like this.
She told me she's planned it all out.
I told her everything she has to live for, all of the
things she has in store.
Her eyes lit up and she started asking questions,
excited and eager to know more.
I told her she'll just have to wait and see for herself,
I can't spoil the ending.
She said she can't wait to be 26 and know all the
incredible moments that make her pain today all
worthwhile.

She doesn't know that I'm hoping in my next dream I
get to meet me at 36, because I'd love to know the
incredible moments that make my pain today all
worthwhile.

But I can't wait to see for myself,
Because I know she wouldn't spoil the ending.

-

In high school, I wanted to kill myself.
I didn't want to wake up and see the girls with
hourglass bodies that I didn't have,
Who yelled names at me in the halls, called me fat
online, and told me everyone would be better off if I
was dead.
I didn't want to wake up and see the boy who was my
first love,
Who caused my dad to rock me in his arms to stop
my crying for the first time since I was a baby.
I didn't want to wake up and see the older boy who
held me like a yo-yo in his hand,
Reeling me in, and throwing me back out to the
sharks more vulnerable than before,
Time and time and time and time again.

In high school, I wanted to kill myself.
I didn't want to wake up and see the girls whose
hourglass bodies haven't held up, who are still as
insecure today as they were then.
I didn't want to wake up and see the boy who was my
first love,
Who was only the first to break my heart, but
nowhere near the last. I'd fall in love many times
since.
I didn't want to wake up and see the older boy who
surely had issues that were never mine to hold,
Whose power didn't go beyond the walls of that
hometown.

In high school, I wanted to kill myself.
And everyday, I'm thankful I lived to see what the
people on my suicide note grew up into.
And everyday, I'm thankful I lived to see myself
become the woman that young girl needed.

I've always chastised my mom for her selflessness.
I've told her it's naive to be so giving to others.
So forgiving to others.
I've preached the importance of not trusting, being
wary of intentions, and always staying guarded.
When really, these are her greatest powers.
She is strong enough to stay vulnerable, loving, and
tender to everyone she meets despite what she's seen
in the world and experienced in her own life.
In reality, I was the naive one to not realize this
sooner.
I pushed my own fears and hesitations onto someone
who's well aware of what possibilities lie ahead, but
knows how to face them with her hands wide open
instead of in fists.

- Compassion is not a detriment, and
not understanding that was mine

Somewhere between then and now,
It went from "Mom, stop telling me what to do."
To "Mom, please tell me what to do."

Somewhere between then and now
It went from "Mom, you don't understand."
To "Mom, I don't understand."

Somewhere between then and now
It went from, "Mom, stop asking so many questions."
To "Mom, I have so many questions."

Somewhere between then and now
It went from "Mom, leave me alone"
To "Mom, never leave my side."

Somewhere between then and now I realized the other half of my heart was always the person who created it in the first place.

- Thank you for passing even a portion of your magic onto me

Out of all the love poems that I've written every
single year,
About lovers, friends, family, or conversations I
overhear,
About people I've never met and places far away
from here,
I realized I never wrote a love poem about the woman
in the mirror.

I never told her how she's gotten me through all of
my worst days,
Or how she's always been worth more than what the
scale says she weighs,
Or how strong it is when she wants so badly to give
up but still she stays,
Or how she doesn't even realize all of the people
she'll amaze.

I've written countless pages about the boys who
broke my heart,
But none about the girl who picks up and fixes every
damaged part,
The one who's never left my side and been my other
half from the start,
The one I didn't even realize deserved to be the muse
of all my art.

She has a way of demanding the attention of every room she enters.

While she's pulling at her clothes to hide flaws only visible to her, I stare at her in awe.

She smiles and jokes with people in a way that makes them feel like they've known her forever, but i can tell that's all just surface level small talk for her.

She's shining like a star for them while hiding endless galaxies within herself.

She broadcasts the version of herself that she thinks will be the most likable,

Most digestible,

Most guarded.

Not realizing that she's enchanting everyone without even showing them the most magical parts of herself.

I came across an old video of us today.
It reminded me that "us" wasn't the love story I made
it out to be.
"Us" wasn't the relationship I see when I look back at
all of our perfectly curated photos and screenshots of
sweet messages that were always just to win me back.
"Us" was me excitedly talking to my friend and you
in the background looking me up and down rolling
your eyes, because surely whatever I was saying that
was making her laugh couldn't have been funny.
Surely whatever I was saying couldn't have been
smart, or worth listening to, or smiling at.
Surely whatever I was saying was just annoying.
"Us" was me being the light in any room and you
being a cloud that loomed over it.
"Us" was nothing more than a parasitic relationship.

*- I stopped romanticizing darkness and
realized how much I like shining*

I think the universe gives us second chances
sometimes.
I think it secretly enjoys watching us face the
parallels.
It places you in situations you've been in before years
later.
Maybe the faces and cities have changed,
Or maybe they haven't.
Either way, it gives you the chance to face the same
obstacles and decisions, as well as the potential
happiness or pain that follows, all over again.
It watches as you have the chance to choose again, if
one is worth the other.

I think the universe gives us second chances
sometimes.
And this time, I'm doing what I should have done the
first time.

- I'm walking away

"Please let me put you back together," he said.
While it's been five days since I could get out of bed,
Or find anything loud enough to silence my head,
But I hand him my heart and some needles and
thread.

"Don't you realize that you deserve happiness?"
he sighed.
But he doesn't know how many 3 am tears that
I've cried,
Over a love that wasn't love and a part of me that
died,
But I force a smile and just say, "Believe me, I've
tried."

"I want to remind you everyday how amazing you
are."
I decided to let him, not thinking he'd get very far,
But he kisses every bruise and is in awe of every scar,
And every day I learn that love doesn't have to be so
hard.

A woman will mold herself perfectly into your life
like sand in the palm of your hand if you let her.
If you hold too tight, she will crumble.
If you don't hold tight enough, she'll slip right
through your fingers.

- Take me as a grain of sand and build me into
a castle

Against my logic, I have to hold out hope that there's somewhere we go after death.
I don't think the love I have for you can be contained in one lifetime.
I think it's found you before and
I think it will find you, again and again,
In every lifetime,
Every universe,
And every afterlife.
My love will find you because you're all it knows.
I will always find you.

- I love you 3000

Even if I lose your clothes,
Your pictures,
Your number,
You will live forever in these pages.

- If a writer loves you, you'll live forever

He wanted me to have less sugar.
The next wanted me to have less cream.
One wanted me to be the perfect mixture in between.

He wanted me to be sweeter,
The next just wanted me to quench his thirst,
One wanted me hotter but didn't want his tongue
burnt.

He wanted me to be watered down,
The next wanted to have me for free,
Then one finally took me as I was and said I was his
perfect cup of tea.

Maybe it's because I'm a Libra.
With my ruling planet being Venus, my ruling
Goddess being Aphrodite,
I was destined to be this way from the beginning of
time. It was written in the stars.
Aphrodite, the Goddess of Love, is said to have
created the rose from the tears and blood of her lover.
I too have made beauty out of tears shed from me and
for me.
I too have torn myself open at the seams for love, and
have managed to continue finding more to give
despite how much I've lost.
I too have always drowned in the idea of love.

I try to look at each love like a sunset.
It goes by quickly,
So quickly that if you blink you might miss it.
It's all-consuming. It turns your entire world shades
of pink and red.
Pictures and words never do it justice,
And nobody experiences it the same way.
No two are identical, but that doesn't make them any
less beautiful.
It leaves you feeling lucky to be alive.
It leaves you feeling total admiration for something
that never has, or will, belong to you,
Then, it leaves you all together.
And you're left with the pictures,
And the words,
And a dark sky.

But it will always be better to have watched the
sunset fade than to have never seen it at all.

You're going to fall.

Hard.

His smile is going to water every part of you and
grow flowers where you didn't even know they could
grow.

You're going to burst into a million butterflies when
he touches you and they're going to flutter in circles
around him wherever he goes.

And honey, he's going to go.

And your butterflies are going to follow.

And your flowers are going to tangle their stems
around his ankles and your roots are going to try and
hold him until they snap.

He'll pick the wings off your butterflies and wade
through the remains of your own garden to free
himself.

You're going to wake up one day in a hole dug by
your own desperation, in the wasteland of a love that
once promised you "forever."

And you're going to cry so hard you could drown.

But the tears are going to be the foundation of a new
garden, with flowers that only you can water.

Slowly, you will rebuild yourself with the love and
nurture that he could never give you and you'll
realize that all the love you needed,

Was within you all along.

I've fallen in love with my sadness and anxiety.
Not in a way I romanticize it, but in a way I've
learned how much I wouldn't want to live without it.
I want to feel heartache and gut-wrenching emptiness
to allow me to know even deeper happiness and
gratitude.
I want to have emotional depth that could drown and
swallow me entirely.
I want sleepless nights and the creativity they bring to
my mind.
While laying awake I used to wish on every star not
to feel so damn deeply about everything,
And now I realized they don't just light up the night
sky, they live within me and light me up from the
inside out,
Even if it burns sometimes.

- It must be boring to not know feelings this deep

It can be hard to look back and realize how far you've
come,
From when you were standing on the wrong side of a
fully loaded gun,
Not only having nightmares but also living inside of
one,
And then one day you wake up and you're
surrounded by the sun.

You see that all the walls have been rebuilt in your
kingdom,
And you're no longer suffering from Stockholm
syndrome,
And these days it seems crazy to think you were ever
a victim,
While you stand tall with pride, beauty, knowledge
and wisdom.

And while sometimes you remember all the things
you went through,
It's only to remind yourself how much you grew,
You dragged yourself out of the well that he threw
you into,
Climbed the highest tree and repainted your own sky
bright blue.

I feel blessed for everything that didn't go my way, and in result, everything that did.

I surrounded myself with people who love me, and they taught me to give the love I was searching for from others to myself. I let laughter cure what time couldn't yet. I figured out that the most important lessons we learn are always the most painful, and that sometimes you have to burn bridges to clear paths. I decided that no matter how much betrayal or toxicity I face, I will never grow bitter or stop putting my love and energy out into the atmosphere, because I know it will come back to me.

I learned that I'm a force to be reckoned with, and if someone doesn't realize that it's not my job to show them. I'm no longer wondering if I'm enough for people, but wondering if they're enough for me.

I'm discovering with no limits, loving more despite the turmoil, laughing harder, dreaming bigger, and moving forward.

Acknowledgements

Thank you to my parents who have held my hands through every bruised knee and heartache, and always taught me the importance of not only staying strong, but staying kind.

Thank you to my friends who have brought laughter induced stomach aches into my life on all of the days I didn't even want to smile, and wiping the tears on the days I couldn't.

Thank you to those who see themselves within this book. Whether you caused nightmares, dreams, or both, you caused inspiration and growth that I can now share with people who need it.

And lastly, thank you to those who need it. Thank you for staying, growing, trying, loving, and reading my cracked open rib cage on these pages. It finally feels like I have someone staying up with me on the nights I can't sleep.

Printed in Great Britain
by Amazon

32932806R00078